The Ideal Muslimah

Things We Don't Talk About

Copyright TX000931710

Al-Aededan

Religion, History, Health, Psychology

All rights reserved. No part of this book may be reproduced or transmitted in any form or by any means, electronic or mechanical, including photocopying, recording, or by any information storage and retrieval system, without written permission from the Publisher.

Contents

Introduction 5

Faith is life itself 9

How does menstruation or postpartum bleeding have an effect on my capacity to worship? 13

What is forbidden to me during my menses or postpartum? 15

Should I make up the prayers that I miss? 17

Can I perform any ablutions during menses or postpartum bleeding (postpartum)? 21

Am I allowed to make any prostration? 25

Must I avoid all acts of worship altogether? 27

How, then, have women been led to extremes in avoiding other acts of worship? 28

Can I read and recite the Qur'an? 29

May I touch or carry the Qur'an? 35

What is the difference between those who are in post-sex impurity and those who are impure due to menstruation or postpartum bleeding? 39

What do I do if I am menstruating or postpartum during Ramadan? 43

Can I perform Hajj? 47

May I enter a masjid (mosque)? 51

Can I attend the Eid prayers? 51

Am I permitted to wash or prepare the dead for burial? 55

How can a woman get closer to Allah? 55

How will a woman know that her menstrual or postpartum period has ended? 61

Once this period ends, what to do? 61

Is Masturbation a sin? 67

The Islamic scholars' opinions 77

The Four Schools of Law in Islam 79

The Hanafiyya School 83

The Malikiyya School 85

The Shafiyya School 87

The Hanbaliyya School 89

Sahfi's and Maliki's Opinion 91

Introduction

In response to the requests of many friends, we have made many revisions to this book. We have added information, particularly about worshiping Allah in Ramadan. In addition, we felt that it was very important to note the availability of more material in English on this subject in the years since the first edition was written and published. This new book is dedicated to 'Umm Omar', who lovingly reminded all people of the importance of imparting beneficial knowledge to everyone. It is one of the three ways the Last Prophet (peace and blessings be upon him) has told us that our good deeds can continue after we leave this life. May Allah accept this effort from her and us all, and may He have mercy on her and grant her paradise for her patience in adversity.

Questions Muslim women ask most often regarding their religion have to do with women issues such as menstruation and also masturbation. If you ask why masturbation is frowned upon in most cultures, then well, pretty much everything related to the female body and sex for-pleasure-only are frowned upon. The only exception is married sex - the kind of sex that is expected to produce children.

Women are also affected by menstruation and often post-childbirth bleeding for regular and prolonged periods in their lives. Islam has specific rules for a woman in these conditions. Sara is a mother and life-long student and has a master's degree in Education. She has been reading about Islam and the subject of the worship of Allah as it affects women since she accepted Islam years ago. She felt that she had many unanswered questions about the topic of worship during the time of a woman's menstruation. More specifically, she had not found many good answers to the questions of whether a menstruating woman could fast, pray, or read the Holy Qur'an.

Sara began to look for answers to her questions in books of fiqh (Islamic jurisprudence). She found a fatwa (religious decree) in the great work of Ibn Taymiyah, al-Fatawa al-Kubra, which stated that it was permitted for a menstruating woman to read the Qur'an. From there Sara started to research the subject in more detail. She wrote a short article outlining what she had learned and kept it in her file until she could find a way to disseminate what she had learned to other women.

Whenever a Muslim, whether a man or woman, has a question about their religion, they should seek the answer in the Qur'an (Allah's revealed Word) and the Sunnah (the example in word and deed) of His Prophet Muhammad (peace and blessings be upon him). If the answer is not found in these two sources, they should look to trustworthy Muslim scholars for help. Everyone is encouraged to read, study, and learn as much as they can about their religion, for the search for religious knowledge is an obligation upon every Muslim individual.

We have sent it down as an Arabic Qur'an, in order that ye may learn wisdom. (Quran 12:2)

If the question is about a subject related to fiqh (which deals with understanding and interpreting the Sharia or Islamic law), they may find more than one simple answer. This is in part because after the death of the Prophet (peace and blessings be upon him) and the end of Revelation, the Companions and those who came after them spread out over the world and became separated by time and space.

This separation came, in a time and era where fast transportation and instant communication did not yet exist. So scholars had to develop their schools of thought in near isolation from each other and, in some cases, far from the sources of the Sunnah.

As a result, the Imams who founded these schools of Islamic thought each developed a different set of opinions and legal decisions to be put into practice by their followers. The four Imams of the major Sunni schools of thought never intended for their opinions to be used to divide and split the Muslim community. In fact, they all said that if anything which they had decreed was not in accordance with the Book of Allah and the Sunnah of His Messenger (peace and blessings be upon him), then it was to be disregarded. Nonetheless, these schools of thought evolved over many centuries into rigid sects. People began following them blindly, and Muslims lost sight of the more important goals of unity in their religion and obedience to Allah and His Prophet (peace and blessings be upon him) above all else.

Every century or so, however, Allah the Exalted has given one or two of His servants the knowledge and wisdom to look beyond the petty divisions and call Muslims back to the straight path.

Faith is life itself

The Messenger of Allah (peace and blessings be upon him) said: *"The best of people is (1) My generation, (2) then those who come after them, (3) then those who come after them." (Bukhari and Muslim)*

These three generations of virtuous Muslims are known as 'the righteous ones who follow' (what has been originally handed down – that is, the Sunnah), while those who followed after the first three generations are often called 'people of the Sunnah'.

The only means of purifying the heart and of removing anxieties and worries from it is to have complete faith in Allah, Lord of all that exists. In fact, there can be no true meaning to life when one has no faith. How base and mean is a life without faith! How eternally accursed is the existence enveloping those who are outside of the boundaries set down by Allah (the Exalted)!

وَنُقَلِّبُ أَفْـِٔدَتَهُمْ وَأَبْصَٰرَهُمْ كَمَا لَمْ يُؤْمِنُوا۟ بِهِۦٓ أَوَّلَ مَرَّةٍ وَنَذَرُهُمْ فِى طُغْيَٰنِهِمْ يَعْمَهُونَ ﴿١١٠﴾

And We shall turn their hearts and their eyes away [from guidance], as they refused to believe therein for the first time, and We shall leave them in their trespass to wander blindly. (Qur'an 6:110)

Has not the time come when the world should have an unquestioning faith – that none has the right to be worshipped except Allah (the Exalted)? After centuries of experience, should not humankind be led to the realization that having faith in a statue is ludicrous, that atheism is absurd, that the Prophets were truthful, and that to Allah alone belongs the dominion of the heavens and earth?

All praise is due to Allah, and He is capable of all things. You will be happy and at peace in proportion to the level of your faith -strong or weak, firm or wavering.

مَنْ عَمِلَ صَـٰلِحًا مِّن ذَكَرٍ أَوْ أُنثَىٰ وَهُوَ مُؤْمِنٌ فَلَنُحْيِيَنَّهُۥ حَيَوٰةً طَيِّبَةً ۖ وَلَنَجْزِيَنَّهُمْ أَجْرَهُم بِأَحْسَنِ مَا كَانُوا۟ يَعْمَلُونَ ﴿٩٧﴾

Whoever works righteousness, whether male or female, while he is a true believer; verily, to him We will give a good life [in this world with respect, contentment, and lawful provision]. And We shall pay them certainly a reward in proportion to the best of what they used to do [that is, paradise in the hereafter]. (Qur'an 16:97)

The 'good life' that is mentioned in this verse refers to having a firm faith in the promise of our Lord and a steady heart that loves Him. People who lead this 'good life' will also have calm nerves when afflicted with hardship; they will be satisfied with everything that befalls them, because it was written for them, and because they are pleased with Allah as their Lord, with Islam as their religion, and with Muhammad as their Prophet and Messenger.

وَنُقَلِّبُ أَفْـِٔدَتَهُمْ وَأَبْصَٰرَهُمْ كَمَا لَمْ يُؤْمِنُوا بِهِۦٓ أَوَّلَ مَرَّةٍ وَنَذَرُهُمْ فِى طُغْيَٰنِهِمْ يَعْمَهُونَ ﴿١١٠﴾

And We shall turn their hearts and their eyes away [from guidance], as they refused to believe therein for the first time, and We shall leave them in their trespass t0 wander blindly. (Qur'an 6:110)

Some of those in the long chain of scholars and thinkers whose work still influences Islamic thought today are al-Ghazâli, Muhammad ibn Rushd, Taqi ad-Deen ibn Taymiyah, Muhammad ibn 'Abdul-Wahhâb, and Hassan al-Banna.

It was al-Banna who commissioned his student and colleague Sayyid Sâbiq to write the now well-known Fiqh us-Sunnah. Contemporary scholars like Sayyid Sâbiq and Muhammad Shawkâni have depended greatly on the legacy of the earlier righteous followers in making known to modern Muslim readers the true nature of the Sunnah.

It is in these scholars' writings as well as in the opinions of the four Imams that we can find the answers to our questions on the topic of worship and menstruation.

How does menstruation or postpartum bleeding have an effect on my capacity to worship?

Believing Muslims who practice their religion sincerely know that worship of Allah takes many forms.

- Ṣalâh (prayer)
- Sadaqah (voluntary charity)
- Dhikr (remembrance of Allah)
- Du'â'
- Studying and reciting the Qur'an
- Istighfâr (asking for forgiveness from Allah)
- Fasting
- I'tikâf (seclusion inside the mosque)
- Zakât (obligatory donations
- Hajj and 'umrah are acts of worship that Muslims perform periodically.

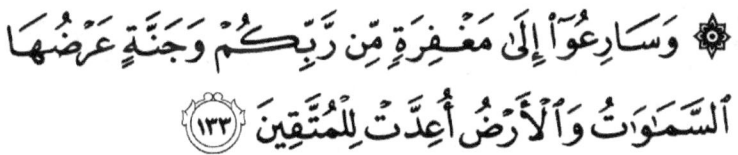

And hasten to forgiveness from your Lord and a garden as wide as the heavens and earth, prepared for the righteous. (Quran 3:33)

A Muslim woman who is learning about her religion finds out quickly that the menstrual period and the period of bleeding after childbirth (postpartum bleeding) are times for her to leave off certain acts of worship such as formal prayer and fasting, as well as specified sexual relations with her husband.

It is important for believing women to be aware of exactly which acts are forbidden and which ones are permitted to them in these situations. This booklet is intended to clear up the issue as much as possible (with Allah's permission).

What is forbidden to me during my menses or postpartum?

The Qur'an and the Sunnah of Allah's Messenger (peace and blessings be upon him) are clear about these restrictions. Allah (the Exalted) says:

$$\text{وَيَسْـَٔلُونَكَ عَنِ ٱلْمَحِيضِ ۖ قُلْ هُوَ أَذًى فَٱعْتَزِلُوا۟ ٱلنِّسَآءَ فِى ٱلْمَحِيضِ ۖ وَلَا تَقْرَبُوهُنَّ حَتَّىٰ يَطْهُرْنَ ۖ فَإِذَا تَطَهَّرْنَ فَأْتُوهُنَّ مِنْ حَيْثُ أَمَرَكُمُ ٱللَّهُ ۚ إِنَّ ٱللَّهَ يُحِبُّ ٱلتَّوَّٰبِينَ وَيُحِبُّ ٱلْمُتَطَهِّرِينَ ﴿٢٢٢﴾}$$

"They ask you concerning menstruation. Say that it is a harmful thing, therefore keep away from [your wives] during menses and do not have sexual intercourse with them until they have become pure [from menstrual blood], and when they have purified themselves [from menses by taking a shower] then you [husbands] may have sexual intercourse with them as Allah has ordained for you." (Qur'an 2:222)

The Messenger of Allah (peace and blessings be upon him) told Fâṭimah bint Abu Ḥubaysh (may Allah be pleased with her):

"When your menses begins, leave off the prayer, and when it has ended, wash the blood from your body and pray."

In Bukhari's version, he said:

"And you (women) are to leave off the prayer for the number of days in which you menstruate, then wash and pray."

Should I make up the prayers that I miss?

As for the prayer, its significance – or rather part of its significance – is that it empties the heart from bad feelings and fills it with strength and pleasure. During prayer, one's heart and soul are in communication with Allah. Closeness to Him, the comfort realized from asking of Him, and the spirituality felt from standing in front of Him – these are all realized during the prayer. Every limb is used in the prayer, but what is more important is that the heart must be wakeful as well. When one prays, tranquility and peace are achieved as one travels away, at least spiritually, from enemies and troubles. Thus the prayer is one of the most potent of remedies for the diseases of the heart. Yet only the worthy heart benefits from prayer; the weak heart, on the other hand, is like the body, in that it seeks its sustenance from material matter. Therefore prayer is the greatest way to help us achieve the blessings of both this world and the hereafter. The prayer precludes one from sins, defends against diseases, illuminates both heart and face, makes one active, and in general, brings good upon the person who performs it sincerely.

In every other hadith, 'Â'ishah bint Abi Bakr (peace and blessing on her), told a lady who had asked about missed prayers:

"The Messenger of Allah (peace and blessings be upon him) said that we have been ordered to make up the fasts (overlooked because of menstruation or postpartum bleeding), and we were ordered now not to make up the prayers." (Bukhari)

If, however, a woman did not pray an obligatory prayer in the beginning of the prescribed time for that prayer, and then her menses began after she would have had enough time to make ablution and pray, she would have to make up that prayer after her menses ends. For example, if the midday prayer started at 12 noon, and by 12:20 she had not started to pray, and then her menstrual blood started to flow, she has missed the midday prayer in its time, and must make it up at the end of her menses. If on the other hand, her period began at 12:05 for example, she would not be obligated to make up the midday prayer later, as there would not have been sufficient time in five minutes to make ablution and pray.

Therefore, a woman who is expecting her menstrual period to start anytime soon should try her best to pray on time, so that she will not miss any of her prayers.

If a woman is in the midst of a prayer (whether obligatory or not), and she feels her menstrual blood starting to flow out, she should immediately stop her prayer. If, however, there is a pressing reason for her not to stop, she may continue the prayer. If she is praying a congregational prayer in a group of worshippers and feels too embarrassed to leave the prayer in the middle, she may complete the prayer. This opinion has been deduced from the scholars' opinion that the excretion of impure substances from the body during one's prayer permits, but does not oblige, the worshipper to leave the prayer without completing it. Then, once her menses has ended, she should repeat that prayer as a missed prayer.

That permission to continue her prayer does not mean, however, that a woman who is already menstruating and is aware of it can join a group prayer simply because she is shy about letting it be known.

To intentionally pray any prayer during one's menses would be a sin, as this is in defiance of Prophet Muhammad's (peace and blessings be upon him) order.

Can I perform any ablutions during menses or postpartum bleeding (postpartum)?

Before I answer this question, some fiqh terms must be explained. Impurities are "substances that the Muslim must avoid and wash off if they happen to contaminate his clothes, body and so on." They include blood, urine, poop, vomit, and many other excretions from the body.

Some of these impurities cause the believer to become 'impure' simply by coming into contact with them. Certain substances excreted from his or her own body also impose a state of impurity.

A Muslim is always either in a state of purity, or of minor impurity, or of major impurity. A state of minor impurity can mean that he or she has passed a bodily fluid, or solid or gas, or that he or she has come into physical contact with some impure substance, or even that the believer was asleep or lost consciousness. In order to purify him or herself from a minor impurity, the Muslim must make ablution (wuḍoo').

According to the majority of the scholars, a state of major impurity means that she or he has had sexual intercourse or emitted a sexual discharge, or that she is menstruating or having postpartum bleeding.

According to the school of thought of Imam Shâfi'i, childbirth (live or still), even without any bleeding postpartum, also puts a woman in a state of major impurity. In order to purify him or herself from a major impurity, a woman must take a complete shower with the intention of purification. Ablution and a ritual shower will return the person from a state of minor or major impurity to a state of purity. The opinion of m scholars of Islamic jurisprudence is that while a woman is in her menses or postpartum, she is not permitted to make ablution or purify herself from it until the discharge has stopped completely, or until the prescribed period for the menses or postpartum bleeding has ended, whichever comes first.

Most scholars say that it is permitted – and actually preferred – however, to perform the ritual shower for purification for other specified reasons, such as putting on the iḥrâm for Hajj or 'umrah, entering Makkah, and standing at Arafat.

The proof that this type of purification is preferred is found in a hadith related by 'Â'ishah (may Allah be pleased with her) that when she was on her way to perform Hajj with the Messenger of Allah (peace and blessings be upon him), her menses began. The Prophet (peace and blessings be upon him) told 'Â'ishah:

"Do what the pilgrims do on Hajj, but do not perform ṭawâf (circumambulation of the Kaaba) until you become pure." (Bukhari)

According to most scholars, it is also permitted for her to take the ritual shower in order to purify herself from the state of post-sex impurity. For example, if a woman had intercourse before the onset of her menstrual period, and then her menstrual blood began to flow before she had made taken a shower, she may still take the shower with the intention of purifying herself from sexual impurity, but without the intention of purifying herself from menses. The Shâfi'i school of thought does not permit the woman who has her menses or the woman who has postpartum bleeding to perform the post-sex ritual purification during the time her discharge is still flowing, but once the discharge has stopped, she may do so.

Things We Don't Talk About

Am I allowed to make any prostration?

Most of the scholars say that the prohibition of performing formal prayer also includes prostration. It is forbidden for anyone to make a prostration upon reciting or hearing a verse of prostration even in a state of minor impurity, as prostration is considered to be like prayer. Therefore it is also forbidden for those in a state of major impurity to do so.

There is some difference of opinion among the scholars of the Sunnah, however, about whether in fact a state of purity is required at all. The prostration of thankfulness also necessitates a state of purity according to some scholars; whereas others say that no prerequisite of purity for the prostration of thankfulness exists, as it is not part of the prayer. In that case, there is nothing to prohibit a woman from making a prostration of thankfulness during her menses or postpartum.

Must I avoid all acts of worship altogether?

In addition to not fasting and not performing prayers, many women have been taught that they may not read the Qur'an, nor recite it or touch it while menstruating. Some women, uneducated as to the extent of the restrictions upon them during this period, go so far as to give up other forms of worship such as the spoken remembrance of Allah, praising Allah and supplication until their menses or postpartum bleeding are over.

Due to a misconception of what is off limits to them, the menstrual and postpartum periods have often meant for many women long periods of non-spirituality, feeling far away from Allah, forgetting parts of the Qur'an which they had memorized, and missing many opportunities for seeking the pleasure of Allah (the Exalted).

There is a great deal of misunderstanding about the acts of worship that are forbidden and those that are permitted to women who are menstruating or postpartum.

The Qur'an and the Sunnah of the Prophet (peace and blessings be upon him) make it clear that the acts of worship expressly forbidden to them are prayer, staying in the mosque and fasting.

How, then, have women been led to extremes in avoiding other acts of worship?

Much of the confusion regarding this matter arises from a tendency by many scholars to classify menstruation and postpartum bleeding together with post-sex impurity as belonging in one and the same category of major impurity. An important example: the section in Sayyid Sâbiq's Fiqh us-Sunnah on 'Acts that are forbidden to the impure' makes no distinction between those who are impure due to menstruation and those who have become impure due to sexual activity. This lack of detailed discussion of the topic in English makes it difficult for any woman to find out what is permissible and what is forbidden to her during her menses or postpartum bleeding.

Can I read and recite the Qur'an?

It is a general principle of Islamic jurisprudence that everything is permissible unless it has been expressly made impermissible.

Scholars of fiqh and the Sunnah – among them Ibn Taymiyah and the late Muhammad ibn Ṣâliḥ 'Uthaymeen – have noted that certainly, women in the time of the Prophet (peace and blessings be upon him) menstruated and gave birth, yet the Messenger of Allah (peace and blessings be upon him) did not make any statements or commands (that can be confirmed as authentic) forbidding them from reading or reciting the Qur'an, or from any form of spoken remembrance of or supplication to Allah.

There is also documentation in Arabic of further clarification of this subject. Ibn Taymiyah, the famous scholar who wrote and taught some 500 years after the Qur'an was revealed, said in his huge work entitled al-Fatâwâ al-Kubrâ (Major Religious Decrees or Decisions), in the chapter on menstruation:

The menstruating woman may read and recite the Qur'an, unlike the one who is in post-sex impurity, and this is in the Mâliki school of thought; and according to Aḥmad (ibn Ḥanbal), if she fears she may forget (what she has memorized or learnt of the Qur'an) then it is obligatory (for her to read and recite it).

In a similar opinion, he said that there were three different views of the scholars on whether a menstruating woman or a person in post-sex impurity could read or recite the Qur'an.

1. It is permissible for both the menstruating woman and the person in post-sex impurity. That was the opinion of Abu Ḥaneefah, and the most well-known opinion of both Shâfi'i and Aḥmad.

2. It is not permissible for a person in post-sex impurity, but is entirely permissible for a menstruating woman.

3. It is permissible for a menstruating woman only if she is afraid of forgetting parts of the Qur'an. That was the opinion of Mâlik, and one of the opinions of Aḥmad and others.

According to Ibn Taymiyah, then, the founders of all of the four major schools of thought, namely, Imam Abu Ḥaneefah Nu'mân ibn Thâbit, Imam Muhammad Shâfi'i, Imam Mâlik ibn Anas and Imam Aḥmad ibn Ḥanbal, are of the opinion that women who are menstruating or having postpartum bleeding may or should read and recite the Qur'an. Imam Shâfi'i, however, holds the view that women in such conditions may not recite out loud any verses of the Qur'an. In support of this opinion, scholars often quote the following weak hadith:

"Abdullâh ibn 'Umar (may Allah be pleased with both of them) related that the Messenger of Allah (peace and blessings be upon him) said: The one who is in post-sex impurity and the one who is menstruating may not recite anything from the Qur'an." (Recorded by Abu Dâwood and at-Tirmidhi)

This hadith as it has been reported has been graded weak by Imam Nawawi as well as by subsequent scholars. The late Shaykh Ibn Bâz, who had been the Mufti of Saudi Arabia, quoted the above hadith and then commented that it was weak, because it came from an unreliable source.

All of the four schools of thought agree that reading without reciting is not forbidden, as long as she does not directly touch the muṣḥaf (the purely Arabic Qur'an which is not mixed with other writing such as explanations of the meaning of the verses). Nevertheless, the major schools of thought and a number of well-known scholars have put certain restrictions on the way in which a woman during her menses or postpartum can read the Qur'an. According to the Mâliki School, she is permitted to recite parts of the Qur'an until and unless her blood has stopped flowing – that is, at the end of the menses or postpartum bleeding – at which time she may not recite until she has taken a ritual shower. The Shâfi'i opinion is that she is permitted to read while moving her tongue, but silently. She may read as much as she needs to for purposes of study or teaching.

According to Imam Shâfi'i, she can also recite verses or chapters for blessing and protection – like Âyat al-Kursi (Qur'an 2:255), Soorat al-Falaq (Qur'an 113), and Soorat an-Nâs (Qur'an 114), but not with the intention of worship or remembrance of Allah.

Despite the tendency of all four schools of thought to put conditions on the permissibility of reciting the Qur'an during menses or postpartum bleeding, there remains the fact that there is no proof from the Qur'an or the Sunnah of Allah's Messenger (peace and blessings be upon him) that a menstruating woman may not recite the Qur'an.

Shaykh Ibn Bâz wrote in his book Fatâwâ (Islamic Decrees) in the chapter 'Decrees about the Qur'an' that (in summary) a woman who is in either of those conditions may read or recite the Qur'an silently or aloud and in any situation. Ibn Bâz states that this is the most correct opinion of the scholars, and that there is nothing from the Prophet (peace and blessing be upon him) which forbids this. She may recite to herself or to others (excluding of course men who are not her closest relatives or her husband) as for example in teaching her children, in a study group, reciting verses before sleeping, as part of her supplication to Allah, studying from books of tafseer (exegesis or explanation of the meanings of the Qur'an) or other books containing Qur'anic verses, and memorizing or reciting verses from the muṣḥaf (purely Arabic Qur'an).

May I touch or carry the Qur'an?

Most scholars, from all the major schools of thought, say that the woman during her menses or postpartum bleeding may not directly touch or carry the muṣḥaf. She may touch it only if it becomes necessary to do so. There are differences of opinion as to which situations indicate necessity. In the Shâfi'i school, the risk to the muṣḥaf of harm from fire or water, or of coming into contact with impurities, all would compel her to pick it up. She is otherwise forbidden from carrying the muṣḥaf even if it were in a bag that she carried, if her intention was expressly to carry the muṣḥaf. The Hanafi School and others consider the need to read from the muṣḥaf itself a necessity, but say that in this case the woman should avoid touching it directly. The majority of scholars agree that touching and holding a copy of the Qur'an which is mixed with tafseer (explanations) or which is not purely in Arabic is acceptable for anyone who is menstruating or in minor impurity. This means, of course, that it is perfectly acceptable for a woman in her menses or postpartum to carry the book which is the Qur'an translated into English, or which has both the Arabic verses and the English translation and explanation included in the same volume.

The Shâfi'i school of thought is in agreement with this opinion, however, makes the condition that the amount of non-Qur'anic material must exceed the amount of Qur'anic verses in the book.

On this issue, we asked an Imam and scholar who studied the Sunnah about touching the Qur'an. He said that the woman who is menstruating or postpartum may use gloves or a piece of cloth, or turn the pages with a pen, for example, if she needs to read from the pure Arabic muṣḥaf itself. The Ḥanafi school of thought agrees with this opinion. This is an important point as many women in the Islamic world cannot afford, or otherwise have no access to, books of tafseer or other scholarly works. Their only option is the family muṣḥaf found in their own homes. Some scholars permit the muṣḥaf to be touched or carried by an impure person if a separable cover or case covers it, and as long as only the cover of the book is touched, and not the inner pages on which the verses are written. There is a scholarly opinion – held by a minority, but with a strong argument for their claims – that even touching or carrying the muṣḥaf is not forbidden to those who are impure, whether due to menstruation, post-childbirth bleeding or post-sexual activity. This view is based on the interpretation of the verses in Soorat al-Wâqi'ah:

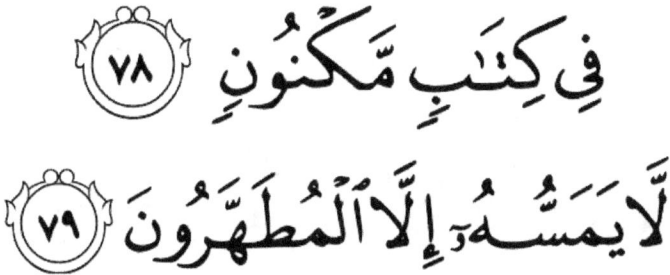

In a book well-guarded, which none can touch but those who are pure. (Qur'an 56:78-79)

Refers to the Book with Allah in Heaven, and 'those who are pure' as referring specifically to the angels, not human beings. Thus, the restriction would not apply to the Qur'an of which we have copies in our hands.

What is the difference between those who are in post-sex impurity and those who are impure due to menstruation or postpartum bleeding?

According to many scholars, among whom are Ibn Bâz and Ibn Taymiyah, the reasons scholars differentiate between a person who is impure because of sexual relations or discharge and a woman who is bleeding from menstruation or postpartum are clear. There are sound hadiths stating that mentioning Allah and reciting the Qur'an were allowed for menstruating women by order of the Messenger of Allah (peace and blessings be upon him). In addition, we know that the Prophet (peace and blessings be upon him) was never kept from mentioning Allah or reciting the Qur'an except by sexual impurity, and this is why scholars have ruled that supplicating and mentioning Allah is disliked for the person in a condition of post-sex impurity. According to some narrations, he expressly forbade reciting even one verse by one who had become impure due to sexual activity until he or she was purified. Ibn Bâz explained that the person who has become impure due to sexual activity usually has control over when and for how long he or she becomes and remains impure, thus the state of impurity continues only for a short period of time.

That person may take a ritual shower or make dry ablution (tayammum) at any time to return to a state of ritual purity. The woman who has become impure due to menstruation or postpartum bleeding, on the other hand, has no control over when and for how long she will be bleeding. The timing and duration of her state of impurity is up to Allah. A woman may be in this state of major impurity for days – or even weeks, in the case of one with postpartum bleeding. A woman in this situation needs to be able to read the Qur'an in order to receive guidance, so that she does not miss the blessings and benefit of the Qur'an, and so as not to forget what she has learned and memorized. We know from the Prophet's hadith and from the opinions of scholars that to intentionally forget what has been memorized and understood of the verses of the Qur'an is a sin.

It is always necessary for Muslim women to have continuous access to the guidance and blessings received by reading and reciting the Qur'an, and this is the most correct opinion of the scholars. The scholars who do not share this opinion differ as to the classification of major impurities.

Imam Shâfi'i and others do make some distinctions between the case of the person who has become impure due to sexual activity and that of the woman who is impure due to menses or postpartum, insofar as the latter two are permitted to read (silently) small chapters and sections of the Qur'an, whereas the former may not. In general, though, these three categories are all considered to be in a state of major impurity, and thus those scholars have forbidden them from reciting the Qur'an. As a result, the strict prohibitions regarding the recitation of the Qur'an by someone in a state of post-sex impurity are also often applied to women in their menses and postpartum, but with some exceptions.

What do I do if I am menstruating or postpartum during Ramadan?

It makes sense that while she may not pray or fast during Ramadan, the woman who is menstruating or bleeding postpartum should be encouraged to do as many other acts of worship as are allowed for her. She is not expected to leave off remembering Allah or praising Him or supplicating to Him at any time of the year. She is not required to give up her daily reading and reciting of the Qur'an. Scholars who hold this view have said that during Ramadan, when the recitation of the Quran is especially encouraged, it is permissible for a woman in her menses or postpartum to continue her reading and reciting, although her prayers and fasting have been interrupted.

The ruling on this issue has been explained in detail in the following fatwa:

Question: *I was wondering what a woman can do on laylat al-qadr if she is menstruating at that time. Can she earn extra rewards for engaging herself in worship? If so, what is permissible for her to do so that night?*

Answer: Praise be to Allah. *A woman who is menstruating may do all acts of worship apart from praying, fasting, circumambulating the Kaaba and doing i'tikâf in the mosque.*

It was narrated that the Prophet (peace and blessings be upon him) used to stay up at night during the last ten nights of Ramadan. Bukhari (2401) and Muslim (1174) narrated that 'Â'ishah (may Allah be pleased with her) said: **"When the last ten nights of Ramadan came, the Prophet (bpuh) would refrain from marital relations, stay up at night and wake his family up."**

Staying up at night is not only for prayer, rather it includes all kinds of acts of worship. This is how the scholars interpreted it.

Al-Ḥâfiz said: "Staying up at night" means staying up to do acts of worship.

An-Nawawi said: "Spending the night staying up to pray etc." He said in 'Awn al-Ma'bood: "i.e., in prayer, dhikr and reciting the Qur'an."

Praying qiyâm is the best act of worship that a person can do on Laylat al-Qadr. Hence the Prophet (peace and blessings be upin him) said:

"Whoever spends the night of Laylat al-Qadr in prayer out of faith and in hope of reward, his previous sins will be forgiven." (Narrated by Bukhari, 1901; Muslim, 760)

Because the woman who is menstruating is not allowed to pray, she can spend the night in doing other acts of worship apart from prayer, such as:

1. Reading or reciting Qur'an.

2. Dhikr – such as saying Subḥân Allâh, lâ ilâha illâ Allâh, al-Ḥamdu Lillâh, etc. She can repeat the words, Subḥân Allâh wal-Ḥamdu Lillâh, wa lâ ilâha illâ Allâh, wa Allâhu akbar (Glory be to Allah, praise be to Allah, there is no god but Allah and Allah is Most Great) and Subḥân Allâh wa bi ḥamdihi, subḥân Allâh il-'Azeem (Glory and praise be to Allah, glory be to Allah the Almighty) etc.

3. Istighfâr (praying for forgiveness), by repeating the phrase Astaghfir-Allâh (I ask Allah for forgiveness).

4. Du'â' (supplication) – she can pray to Allah and ask Him for what is good in this world and in the hereafter, for du'â' is one of the best acts of worship.

The Prophet (bpuh) said, *"Du'â' is 'ibâdah (worship)."*

(Narrated by Tirmidhi, 2895; classed as saheeh by Shaykh al-Albâni in Saheeh at-Tirmidhi, 2370)

The woman who is menstruating can do these acts of worship and others on Laylat al-Qadr.

Can I perform Hajj?

There are many other acts of worship which are permissible for menstruating and postpartum women. These include performing the Hajj and 'umrah (minor pilgrimage), of which only the rites of prayer, ṭawâf (circumambulating the Kaaba), and staying within the bounds of the sanctuary of the Kaaba are forbidden to them.

The reason that a menstruating woman is not allowed to perform ṭawâf is because ṭawâf is a form of ṣalât, as explained by the following hadith:

"Ṭawaf around the House is ṣalât, but Allah permitted speaking during it. So whoever speaks should say only good things." (Recorded by at-Tirmidhi, and authenticated by al-Albâni)

In another hadith, the Messenger of Allah (bpuh) told women what to do if they were menstruating or postpartum during Hajj: 'Â'ishah (may Allah be pleased with her) narrated:

"We [all of the Prophet's (peace and blessings be upon him) wives] accompanied him during his (Farewell) Pilgrimage. When we reached Sarif (shortly before arriving at Makkah), my menses started. When the Prophet (peace and blessings be upon him) came to me, I was weeping. He asked: What makes you weep? I replied: I wish I had not come for Hajj this year. He inquired: Perhaps you have got your menses? I replied: Yes. He said: Indeed, this is something that Allah has ordained for the daughters of Adam. So do as other pilgrims do, but do not circumambulate the House (perform ṭawâf) or pray until you are purified (of the menses)." (Bukhari)

In another narration about the incident, 'Â'ishah narrated:

"In the last Hajj of Allah's Messenger (peace and blessings be upon him), I assumed the iḥrâm for Hajj along with Allah's Messenger (peace and blessings be upon him). I was one of those who intended tamattu' (by assuming iḥrâm for 'umrah first, and once completed, coming out of that iḥrâm and then assuming another iḥrâm for the performance of Hajj from Makkah, without bringing a sacrificial animal) and so I did not take the animal with me.

I got my menses and was not clean (the menses continued) until the night before the day of Arafat. I said: O Messenger of Allah! It is the night before the day of Arafat and I intended to perform hajj at-tamattu' with 'umrah. Allah's Messenger (peace and blessings be upon him) told me to undo my hair (to wash it in the ritual shower after menses) and comb it and to postpone the 'umrah. I did so and completed the Hajj. On the night of al-Ḥasbah (a place outside Makkah where the pilgrims go after completing the rites of Hajj at Mina) he ordered 'Abdur-Raḥmân ('Â'ishah's brother) to take me to at-Tan'eem to assume the iḥrâm for 'umrah instead of that of hajj at-tamattu' which I had intended to perform." (Bukhari)

These hadiths also point to the way in which we should accept menstruation as a natural occurrence, not trying to avoid it or getting upset about it, and that we ought to simply make the necessary adjustments to our routine of worship when menses does occur. A question was posed to Shaykh Ibn Bâz: *"Is it permissible or not for the woman who is either menstruating or bleeding postpartum to recite from books of supplications on the day of (standing at) Arafat even though they contain Qur'anic verses?"*

Ibn Bâz wrote in reply:

"There is no blame on the woman in that situation for reciting the supplications prescribed for the 'sacrifices' or required actions of the Hajj, or for that matter, for reciting from the Qur'an itself, for the prohibition is meant only for the one in post-sex impurity, that he should not recite the Qur'an, from a hadith narrated by 'Ali (may Allah be pleased with him)." «'Ali stated that nothing kept the Messenger of Allah (peace and blessings be upon him) from the Qur'an save being sexually impure."

May I enter a masjid (mosque)?

According to many scholars, it is forbidden for women who are menstruating or bleeding after childbirth as well as for people who have not purified themselves after sexual activity to stay inside any masjid (including the Sacred Masjid of the Kaaba), but there is no harm in their passing through it on their way. This means, of course, that the other act of worship forbidden to women in this condition is i'tikâf, or seclusion in the mosque. The Ḥanbali school of thought, however, permits the menstruating (or postpartum) woman to sit inside the mosque once her blood has stopped flowing, even before she has taken the ritual shower, if she has made ablution by wuḍoo'.

Can I attend the Eid prayers?

Attendance of the Eid prayers and listening there to the Eid sermon is always recommended for all women – including menstruating women and of course, women in postpartum.

In a hadith by Ḥafṣah bint Seereen: *"We used to forbid our young women to go out for the two Eid prayers. A woman came and stayed at the palace of Bani Khalaf, and she told us about her sister whose husband had taken part in twelve battles along with the Prophet (peace and blessings be upon him), and her sister had been with her husband in six (of those twelve battles). She (the sister) had said: We used to treat the wounded and look after the patients. Once I asked the Prophet (peace and blessings be upon him): Is there any harm for any of us to stay at home if she does not have an outer garment (to veil herself)? He said: She should cover herself with her sister's (in Islam) outer garment and should participate in the good deeds and in the religious gathering of the Muslims. (Ḥafṣah said:) When Umm 'Aṭiyah came, I asked her whether she had heard this from the Prophet (peace and blessings be upon him). She replied: Yes, may my father be sacrificed for him! [Whenever she mentioned the Prophet (bpuh) she used to say that.] I have heard the Prophet (peace and blessings be upon him) say: The unmarried young girls, the mature unmarried women who screen themselves from the public view, and the menstruating women should come out and participate in the good deeds as well as the religious gathering of the faithful believers. Those who are menstruating should keep away from the prayer area. (Ḥafṣah asked:) Even the menstruating women? (Umm 'Aṭiyah replied:] Does a menstruating woman not stand at Arafat and so forth (that is, participate in other religious activities)?" (Bukhari)*

In a similar hadith, Umm 'Aṭiyah reported:

"We were ordered to go out with the single and menstruating women to the two Eids in order to witness the good and the supplications of the Muslims. The menstruating women would be separated from the others." (Bukhari and Muslim)

The separation of the women in their menses and postpartum from the rest of the worshippers is easily accomplished if the Eid prayer is performed outdoors or in a place other than a mosque (such as an open field, an arena or a stadium). If the prayer is held in a mosque, however, then the opinion of the scholars is that the women in this condition of impurity must remain outside the areas of the mosque that have been designated for prayer, and apart from those who are praying.

Am I permitted to wash or prepare the dead for burial?

Yes women who are menstruating or bleeding postpartum may wash and shroud the dead, or assist others in doing so. The scholar Ibn Qudâmah wrote in his well-known fiqh book al-Mughni that it is permitted for the menstruating woman, as well as for one who is impure after sexual activity, to perform the washing and shrouding of the dead, although it is preferable that this important religious rite be performed by one who is in a state of purity.

How can a woman get closer to Allah?

Once women know the facts about which actions are allowed and forbidden during their menses and postpartum bleeding, they should encourage each other not to neglect these important acts of worshipping Allah. From a hadith narrated by Abu Sa'eed Khudri: *"The Messenger of Allah (peace and blessings be upon him) once passed by a group of women on his way to offer the Eid prayer and said: O women! Give in charity, as I have seen that the majority of the dwellers of hellfire were you (women). They asked: Why is that, O Messenger of Allah? He replied:*

You curse frequently and are ungrateful to your husbands. I have not seen anyone more lacking in intelligence and religion. A cautious, sensible man could be led astray by some of you. The women asked: O Messenger of Allah, what is deficient in our intelligence and religion? He said: Is the evidence of a woman (in witnessing a debt contract) not equal to half that of a man's? They replied: It is. He said: That is where you are deficient in intelligence. Is it not true that a woman in her menses neither prays nor fasts? The women replied: It is. He told them: That is where you are deficient in your religion." (Bukhari)

The meaning of this hadith could not be clearer. The period of time during which a woman neither prays nor fasts is potentially a period in which her faith and worship are in jeopardy. The rewards and benefits of ablution and prayer are missing at this time. Abu Hurayrah (may Allah be pleased with him) narrated that the Messenger of Allah (peace and blessings be upon him) said: *"When a Muslim makes his ablutions and washes his face the water carries away all sins committed by his eyes, and when he washes his hands the water carries away all sins committed by his hands, and when he washes his feet the water carries away all sins towards which he had walked, and he emerges cleansed of all his sins."* (Muslim)

In another narration by Abu Hurayrah, the Prophet (peace and blessings be upon him) said: *"The five daily prayers, two Friday congregational prayers, and observing the fast during two Ramadans atone for whatever may be between them so long as major sins are guarded against." (Muslim)*

When one is not able to perform ablution and prayers, the small sins that accumulate are not being washed away or erased. If women sit back and 'take a vacation' from their worship during their menses and after giving birth, they are giving Satan an easy access to their minds and hearts. Therefore, while they are not praying the prescribed prayers, they can and should still be striving to be as close to Allah as is possible. Even though they are not required to get up in the middle of the night, it is highly recommended. According to a scholar of the Sunnah, the following hadith applies to women in their menses and postpartum as well as to all other believers: *"The Messenger of Allah (peace and blessings be upon him) said: Allah descends to the lowest heaven every night during the last third of the night and says: Who will call on Me so that I may respond to him? Who is asking something of Me so I may give it to him? Who is turning in repentance to Me so I may turn to him in acceptance of it?" (Bukhari, Muslim, and Aḥmad)*

While they do not have to get up at fajr (dawn) for prayer, the female servants of Allah will still (by Allah's will) get rewarded for waking up to seek Allah's forgiveness, remembering Allah with their tongues and on their fingers (saying Subḥân Allâh, Alḥamdulillâh, Allâhu akbar), and reading and reciting the Qur'an.

أَقِمِ ٱلصَّلَوٰةَ لِدُلُوكِ ٱلشَّمْسِ إِلَىٰ غَسَقِ ٱلَّيْلِ وَقُرْءَانَ ٱلْفَجْرِ إِنَّ قُرْءَانَ ٱلْفَجْرِ كَانَ مَشْهُودًا ۝

"Verily, the recitation of the Quran in the early dawn is ever witnessed (attended by the angels in charge of mankind of the day and the night)." (Qur'an 17:78)

Women who feel that they must not recite the Qur'an while postpartum or during their menses should at least continue and even increase their remembrance of Allah. The Almighty has said:

وَٱذْكُر رَّبَّكَ فِى نَفْسِكَ تَضَرُّعًا وَخِيفَةً وَدُونَ ٱلْجَهْرِ مِنَ ٱلْقَوْلِ بِٱلْغُدُوِّ وَٱلْءَاصَالِ وَلَا تَكُن مِّنَ ٱلْغَٰفِلِينَ ۝

"And remember your Lord within yourself in humility and in fear without being apparent in speech - in the mornings and the evenings. And do not be among the heedless." (Qur'an 7:205)

When she hears the call to prayer, she should respond with the words and the supplication that our Prophet (peace and blessings be upon him) taught us to say. While other members of her household are in prayer, she can sit quietly and remember Allah with thankfulness, praises, and supplication. Abu Hurayrah (may Allah be pleased with him) narrated that the Messenger of Allah (peace and blessings be upon him) said:

"There are two phrases that are easy on the tongue, but are heavy on the scales (that weigh the good deeds on the Day of Judgment) and are loved by the Most Merciful: Glorified be Allah, and His is the Praise; Glorified be Allah, the Owner of Majesty (Subḥân Allâh wa biḥamdih and Subḥân Allâh al-'Adheem)." (Bukhari and Muslim)

In another hadith narrated by Abu Hurayrah, the Prophet (peace and blessings be upon him) said: *"One who recites: There is none worthy of worship save Allah the One, Who has no partner, His is the Kingdom and His is the Praise and He has Power over all things, a hundred times during the day will have merit equal to that of freeing ten slaves, and a hundred good deeds will be credited to him, and a hundred of his defaults (sins) will be wiped out, and *he will be safeguarded against Satan till the end of the day; and no one will exceed him in doing good except one who recites these phrases more often than he does.» (Bukhari and Muslim)*

The Messenger (peace and blessings be upon him) also said:

"The defaults (sins) of one – even if they be as the foam of the sea – will be wiped out if he recites a hundred times in the day: Glorified be Allah, and to Him is due all praise." (Bukhari and Muslim)

How will a woman know that her menstrual or postpartum period has ended?

For women who have questions regarding the duration of their menstrual or postpartum discharge, the length of their cycles, or what to do if the discharge lasts longer than is normal, please consult the chapter on 'Menstruation' in Fiqh us-Sunnah, volume one, where this subject is discussed in detail.

Once this period ends, what to do?

Allah (the Exalted) says in the Qur'an:

وَيَسْـَٔلُونَكَ عَنِ ٱلْمَحِيضِ قُلْ هُوَ أَذًى فَٱعْتَزِلُوا۟ ٱلنِّسَآءَ فِى ٱلْمَحِيضِ وَلَا تَقْرَبُوهُنَّ حَتَّىٰ يَطْهُرْنَ فَإِذَا تَطَهَّرْنَ فَأْتُوهُنَّ مِنْ حَيْثُ أَمَرَكُمُ ٱللَّهُ إِنَّ ٱللَّهَ يُحِبُّ ٱلتَّوَّٰبِينَ وَيُحِبُّ ٱلْمُتَطَهِّرِينَ ﴿٢٢٢﴾

"They ask you concerning menstruation. Say: that is an Adha (a harmful thing for a husband to have a sexual intercourse with his wife while she is having her menses), therefore keep away from women during menses and go not unto them till they have purified (from menses and have taken a bath).

And when they have purified themselves, then go in unto them as Allah has ordained for you (go in unto them in any manner as long as it is in their vagina). Truly, Allah loves those who turn unto Him in repentance and loves those who purify themselves (by taking a bath and cleaning and washing thoroughly their private parts, bodies, for their prayers)" (Qur'an 2:222)

The scholars agree that having intercourse before the menstrual or postpartum discharge has stopped, or before the prescribed period of menstruation or postpartum bleeding has ended, is a sin. This is based on the âyah mentioned above, and on a hadith in which: The Messenger of Allah (peace and blessings be upon him) was asked:

"What is allowed for me (to do) with my wife when she is in her menses? He answered: (Allowed) for you is what is above the waist cloth." (Recorded by Abu Dâwood and an-Nasâ'i; authenticated by al-Albâni)

The scholars differ somewhat on the question of whether or not intercourse is permitted once the discharge has stopped, but before the woman makes her complete ablution (the shower) from menstruation. The Mâliki school as well as those of the Shâfi'i and the Ḥanbali agree that sexual intercourse, and touching in a sexual manner what is between the woman's navel and her knees, are both prohibited until she has taken a ritual shower; and this is based on the above hadith and the definition of the term in verse 222 of Surat al-Baqarah, taṭahhurna, as meaning 'purified themselves by the ritual shower.' The Ḥanafi school and the Shâfi'i make the exception that if her menses has lasted ten days or more, the couple may have intercourse once her discharge has stopped – or if it stops and starts again and stops again – before she makes that complete ablution; but if the menses has lasted less than ten days, then she must take her shower before they have intercourse.

Aishah said: *"The Messenger of Allah (peace and blessings be upon him) said to me: Give up the prayer when your menses begins, and when it has finished, wash the blood off your body (take a shower) and start praying."* (Bukhari)

The consensus of the scholars is that a complete ritual shower is required at the end of menstruation or postpartum bleeding, both for prayer and before sexual intercourse. However, according to the scholars, a woman may purify herself from menstruation and sexual activity with one shower for both, if she has the intention for both of them. The scholars base this opinion on the Prophet's (peace and blessings be upon him) saying:

"All acts are based on intentions." (Bukhari)

From this statement of the opinion of the scholars, it can be inferred that sexual intercourse may take place before the complete shower of purification from menstruation. The first thing a woman should do once she has taken her shower, and the most beloved act to Allah, is to pray. If she had missed a prayer that was due on her at the time her menses began, she should make up that prayer first. If, however, the time for the established prayer (the one that is currently due) is almost over (say, time for the midday prayer is nearly over and the afternoon prayer time will begin in a few minutes), then she should pray the current prayer in its time, without delay, and then the missed prayer.

Once a woman has informed herself correctly about menstruation and postpartum bleeding, she can begin to prepare herself for these conditions which recur during her life cycle. She should prepare mentally and spiritually by increasing her reading, reciting and memorizing of the Qur'an, of supplications, and of remembrance of Allah. She no longer needs to feel cut off and far away from Allah at these otherwise difficult periods of her life.

Is Masturbation a sin?

The term "masturbation" refers to the act of releasing one's sexual energy through the act of orgasm. Masturbation is not explicitly forbidden in the Qur'an or the Prophet's hadith. Although some Muslims believe that masturbating is haram, this is not a universally held view. There are a variety of viewpoints on this issue. There are many schools of thought on whether or not it is acceptable, with some saying it is haram and others saying it is disliked (makruh). There are those who believe that protecting one's own private parts is a form of self-defense. Oral sex is another topic that is frequently referred to be haram, however, there are no explicit directives stating that oral sex is haram. However, you can catch STI from having oral sex. And getting certain oral STIs can increase your overall risk of developing oral cancer later in life. There is some degree of risk in leaving any oral STI undiagnosed and, therefore, untreated.

Intercourse during menstruation and anal sex are considered haram and sinful by the Prophet, peace and blessings be upon him.

Oral sex and masturbation may have been left unsaid since they need interpretation based on context if the Prophet, peace and blessings be upon him, got that explicit and didn't address them. Allah is the only one who truly understands what is best. The Islamic view on masturbation is complex, and it is not fair to state that all incidents of masturbating are sinful or haram. There are a plethora of Islamic viewpoints, therefore I advise you to dig further. Masturbation is permitted in some situations and it is better than committing Zina. Ahmad ibn Hanbal and Ibn Qayaam al Jazawi, for example, had this view. Islamic legal tradition treats any sexual contact outside a legal marriage as a crime. The main category of such crimes is zina, defined as any act of illicit sexual intercourse.

ٱلزَّانِيَةُ وَٱلزَّانِى فَٱجْلِدُوا۟ كُلَّ وَٰحِدٍ مِّنْهُمَا مِا۟ئَةَ جَلْدَةٍ وَلَا تَأْخُذْكُم بِهِمَا رَأْفَةٌ فِى دِينِ ٱللَّهِ إِن كُنتُمْ تُؤْمِنُونَ بِٱللَّهِ وَٱلْيَوْمِ ٱلْـَٔاخِرِ وَلْيَشْهَدْ عَذَابَهُمَا طَآئِفَةٌ مِّنَ ٱلْمُؤْمِنِينَ ﴿٢﴾

Those who fornicate – whether female or male – flog each one of them with a hundred lashes. And let not tenderness for them deter you from what pertains to Allah's religion, if you do truly believe in Allah and the Last Day; and let a party of believers witness their punishment. (Qur'an 24:2)

Things We Don't Talk About

$$\text{اَلزَّانِي لَا يَنكِحُ إِلَّا زَانِيَةً أَوْ مُشْرِكَةً وَالزَّانِيَةُ لَا يَنكِحُهَا إِلَّا زَانٍ أَوْ مُشْرِكٌ ۚ وَحُرِّمَ ذَٰلِكَ عَلَى الْمُؤْمِنِينَ ﴿٣﴾}$$

Let the fornicator not marry any except a fornicatress or idolatress and let the fornicatress not marry any except a fornicator or an idolater. That is forbidden to the believers. (Qur'an 24:3)

$$\text{وَالَّذِينَ يَرْمُونَ الْمُحْصَنَاتِ ثُمَّ لَمْ يَأْتُوا بِأَرْبَعَةِ شُهَدَاءَ فَاجْلِدُوهُمْ ثَمَانِينَ جَلْدَةً وَلَا تَقْبَلُوا لَهُمْ شَهَادَةً أَبَدًا ۚ وَأُولَٰئِكَ هُمُ الْفَاسِقُونَ ﴿٤﴾}$$

Those who accuse honorable women (of unchastity) but do not produce four witnesses, flog them with eighty lashes, and do not admit their testimony ever after. They are indeed transgressors. (Qur'an 24:4)

As a result, it is a matter of context. Personally, I do not consider masturbation to be haram, and I feel that it can be a means to safeguard many young people from exposure to pornography, overly sexualized media, and other forms of zina that are readily available in various communities. If you take the position that masturbation is permissible, then take heed of the following points:

1 – As with anything, too much of a good thing may be harmful. Do not overindulge or make it a habit to the point that you become reliant on it. It may become an addiction, and some individuals grow furious and irritated if they do not masturbate on a daily basis for the delightful release. It can develop the same drug dependence.

2 – Do not masturbate with blatantly haram objects like as pornography. Masturbation between couples does not qualify as masturbation. This is a sort of foreplay in which couples touch or arouse each other's private areas. Again, married spouses are free to do whatever they wish to fulfill their sexual desires as long as it is agreeable between the two of them and not one of the two plainly prohibited activities expressly mentioned by the Prophet, peace be upon him.

3 – Ibn Qayum al-Jawazi stated that the discharge of sperm is beneficial and should not be ignored for extended periods of time since it might alter emotions badly and helps produce better sperm. Some Islamic scholars believe that masturbation is allowed in tough situations if one fears zina or cannot marry.

5 – We should also fast when feasible, but this does not exclude the use of both fasting and masturbation to protect ourselves against zina and pornography. Because masturbation breaks your fast, you cannot do both at the same time, but you can alternate if your situation is severe and necessitates both.

6 – Recognize that many Islamic viewpoints were established centuries ago, and that concerns are sometimes not addressed in the contemporary context. As a result, one should seek information and investigate not just historical stances, but also modern perspectives, because periods and conditions change.

Advice on how to give up masturbation

In terms of treating the habit of masturbation, we suggest the following:

1- The primary reason for seeking a cure for this condition is to obey Allah and His commandments and to avoid His wrath.

2- Marriage, as soon as possible, is a permanent and speedy solution for this condition, as demonstrated by the Prophet's (peace and blessings be upon him) hadith.

3- Keeping oneself busy with what is good for this world and the afterlife is vital in breaking this habit before it becomes an addiction or it will be very difficult to eradicate.

4- Lowering one's eyes (from looking at forbidden photos, movies, etc.) will assist suppress the urge before it leads to the haram (forbidden). Allah commands men and women to lower their eyes.

5- Investing one's free time in praying and expanding one's Islamic understanding.

6- Being cautious not to acquire any of the medical symptoms associated with masturbation, such as a weakened heart and neurological system, poor vision. More crucially, emotions of worry and guilt, especially when skipping the required prayers due to the necessity to shower after every occurrence of masturbation, especially in the winter, as well as the termination of the fast.

7- Avoiding the misunderstanding masturbation is allowed because it keeps you from engaging in illicit sexual activities like as adultery or even homosexuality.

8- Strengthening one's willpower and resisting the devil, as suggested by the Messenger of Allah (peace and blessings be upon him) when he stated, *"Do not spend the night alone." (Ahmad 6919)*

9- Following the Prophet's (peace and blessings be upon him) aforementioned hadith and fasting as much as possible, because fasting will temper and moderate one's sexual drive. However, one should never overreact and pledge by Allah that they will never to return to the act, because if one does not keep one's word, one will face the consequences of failing to live up to one's oath to Allah.

It is also worth noting that taking drugs and medicines to suppress one's sexual desire is often forbidden because it might permanently impair one's health.

10- Attempting to follow the Prophet's (peace and blessings be upon him) advice on bedtime etiquette, such as reciting the Qur'an and reciting some supplications.

11- Striving hard to be patient and chaste, because persistence, Allah willing, will lead to attaining those good qualities as second nature, as the Prophet (peace and blessings be upon him) explained: *If one falls into this sin, they must hasten to repent, asking forgiveness from Allah, doing good deeds, and not losing hope and feeling despair; these are all prerequisites to curing this problem. It is important to note that losing hope is one of the primary crimes punished by Allah.*

The Islamic scholars' opinions

As far as the act of masturbation is concerned the scholars in Islam have many different opinions:

- The majority of the Islamic scholars say that masturbation in Islam is haram

- However, there is still a large number which also say that it is makruh (discouraged)

- There is another large number of scholars who say that it is mubah.

Mubah is commonly translated as "neutral" or "permitted" in English. "Indifferent" or "(merely) permitted". It refers to an act that is not mandatory, recommended, reprehensible or forbidden, and thus involves no judgment from God.

It is optional so I would like to say at the outset that the majority of the scholars in terms of percentage majority say that it is haram.

However, a large number of scholars may not be the majority, but still the number is huge, say it is makruh. It is discouraged & another large number, though not in majority, they say that it is mubah.

I will discuss these issues more in detail and I will let you know which group of scholars I agree with towards the end.

The Four Schools of Law in Islam

The Holy Qur'an, Tradition and Ijtihad are the three main sources of Islamic law which govern and regulate all aspects of a Muslim's public and private life.

These laws relate to religious worship, prohibitions, and all contracts and obligations that arise in social life such as inheritance, marriage, divorce, punishments, conduct of war and the administration of the state. The science of these religious laws is called Fiqah and the expert in this field such as a jurist is called a faqih (plural: fuqaha). We read that Ijtihad, or the exercise of judgment, is a valid source of Islamic laws in areas where the Holy Qur'an and the Traditions are not explicit. But the exercise of this independent judgment can only be left in the hands of proper scholars of the Holy Qur'an and the Tradition.

The vast majority of Muslims give this right of independent reasoning to only four ancient Muslim theologians and jurists who lived in the first three centuries of Islam. These four fuqaha are:

- Imam Abu Hanifa of Kufa
- Imam Malik bin Anas of Medinah
- Imam Muhammad al-Shafi of Medinah
- Imam Ahmad bin Hanbal of Baghdad

Although a number of other jurists also became popular during their times, only the above four are now recognized by the vast majority of Sunni Muslims. These four great jurists and theologians tried to systemize the Islamic law into a comprehensive rational system which covered all possible legal situations. The four prominent schools of Islamic law are named after their founders and are called the Hanafiyya, the Malikiyya, the Shafiyya, and the Hanbaliyya schools of religious law.

Most Muslims regard these four schools as equally valid interpretations of the religious law of Islam. These schools are in good agreement on all essential aspects of the religion of Islam.

They all acknowledge the authority of the Holy Qur'an and the Traditions as the ultimate source of the Islamic law. Only in areas and situations where these two sources are silent, do the four schools use their independent reasoning in which they may differ with each other.

1. The Hanafiyya School

The earliest school formed was by Imam Abu Hanifa (699-767 A.D.) of Kufa. It generally reflects the views of the jurists of Iraq. Abu Hanifa did not compose or write any books on law himself, but his numerous discussions and opinions as recorded by his disciples, form the basis of this school.

As a theologian and a religious lawyer, Abu Hanifa exercised considerable influence in his time. His legal thought is very consistent, uses high degree of reasoning, avoids extremes, and lays great emphasis on the ideas of the Muslim community.

The Ahmadi Muslims generally follow the Hanafiyya School of law. Other areas in which this school has a following include Turkey, the countries of the Fertile Crescent, Lower Egypt and India.

2. The Malikiyya School

The next school of law in order of time was the one founded by Imam Malik bin Anas (d. 795 A.D.) of Medinah and reflects the views and practices associated with that city.

Imam Malik served as a judge in Medinah and compiled all his decisions in a book form called al-Muwatta (the Leveled Path).

Like the jurists of Iraq, Imam Malik preferred to depend more on the Traditions associated with the Companions of the Holy Prophet.

The adherents of this school are predominantly in North African countries.

3. The Shafiyya School

The third school was founded by Imam al-Shafi (d. 820 A.D.) who was a disciple of Imam Malik.

Imam Shafi placed great importance on the Traditions of the Holy Prophet Muhammad, may peace and blessings of Allah be upon him, and explicitly formulated the rules for establishing the Islamic law. He was a great thinker, had an unusual grasp of principles and a clear understanding of the judicial problems.

This school is strong in Lower Egypt, Syria, India and Indonesia.

4. The Hanbaliyya School

This school was founded by Imam Ahmad bin Hanbal (d. 855 A.D.) of Baghdad. Imam Hanbal did not establish a separate school himself; this was rather done by his disciples and followers.

The Hanbaliyya was the most conservative of the four schools. Its rigidity and intolerance eventually caused its decline over the years. In the eighteenth century, however, this school was revived with the rise of Wahhabism and the growing influence of the House of Sa'ud. Today, Hanbaliyya School is followed only in Saudi Arabia.

The Hanbalis insist on the literal injunctions of the Holy Qur'an and the Hadith and are very strict in the observance of religious duties.

Although the Muslims generally apply the Islamic law according to the principles and details laid down by the four ancient jurists, legal situations keep arising from time to time for which there are no clear answers in these early schools of law. To cope with this changing aspect of Islamic society, particularly in the light of new facts, specialists in the field of Islamic law are asked to give their decisions using the traditional tools of legal science. Such a decision is called a fatwa and the religious scholar who gives this decision is called a mufti.

Sahfi's and Maliki's Opinion

As far as the jurist, the Fiqah amongst the al-Shafi, and the Maliki almost all of them say that masturbation is haram and according to Imam Muhammad al-Shafi of Medinah, may Allah have mercy on him, he says it is haram and he quotes the verse of the Qur'an from Surat Al-Mu'minūn (The Believers), chapter number 23, verse number 5, 6, and 7. However, let me explain these verses, 1 to number 7, from Surat Al-Mu'minūn.

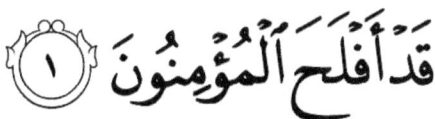

Successful indeed are the believers. (Qur'an 23:1)

Those who offer their Salat (prayers) with all solemnity and full submissiveness. (Qur'an 23:2)

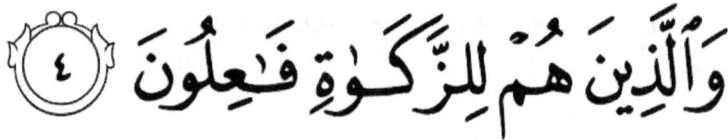

And those who turn away from Al-Laghw (dirty, false, evil vain talk, falsehood, and all that Allah has forbidden). (Qur'an 23:3)

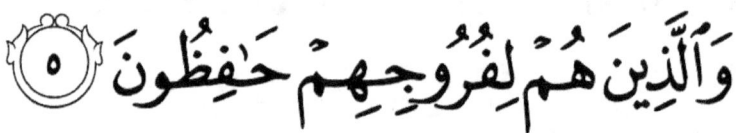

And those who pay the Zakat. (Qur'an 23:4)

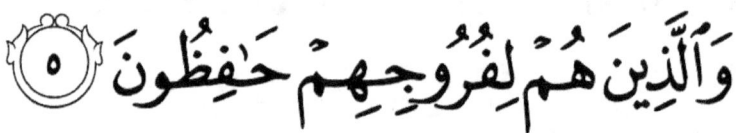

And those who guard their chastity (i.e. private parts, from illegal sexual acts) (Qur'an 23:5)

Except from their wives or (the captives and slaves) that their right hands possess, for then, they are free from blame. (Qur'an 23:6)

But whoever seeks beyond that, then those are the transgressors. (Qur'an 23:7)

If you read these verses carefully

- Verse number 1 says that the believers will eventually be successful.

- Verse number 2 says those who humble themselves in prayers.

- Verse number 3 says those who avoid vain talks.

- Verse number 4 says that those who do acts and deeds of charity.

- Verse number 5 says those who guard their private parts or those who abstain from sex.

- Verse number 6 says but those who they have married or (the captives and slaves) that their right hands possess, for then, they are free from blame.

- Verse number 7 says that all those who cross these limits they are transgressors.

So here the Holy Qur'an says in Surat Al-Mu'minūn (The Believers) number 23, verse number 5, 6 and 7 that the believers are those who guard their private parts and abstain from illicit sex except from their spouses and what their right hand possesses that is an exception. And all those who cross these limits, they are transgressors.

So based on these verses of the Holy Qur'an, Imam Muhammad al-Shafi says the matter is very clear-cut. Sex can only happen with your spouse and what your right hand possesses, and everything else is prohibited.

However, these verses of the Glorious Qur'an can be interpreted in different ways.

The first group of scholars say that they understand these verses as guarding the private parts, which in Arabic means all types of sexual pleasure.

Therefore, this means all types of sexual pleasures. Therefore, for Al-Mu'minūn (The Believer), he or she is only permitted with their wife or husband, and what their right hand possesses, that is the slave girl. However, the slave woman has been abolished. Therefore, the man is restricted to only his wife.

So based on these verses, if all sexual pleasure is only permitted with their spouse, therefore scholars say even masturbation is haram.

However, the other group of scholars say that these verses guard your private parts is only restricted to sexual intercourse. Therefore, the verse of the Holy Qur'an actually means that you can have sexual intercourse only with your wife and what your right hand possesses. So other than sexual intercourse this verse does not refer to other things. So if you agree with the second group of scholars then masturbation does not fall under these verses of the Glorious Qur'an. This is the reason the scholars are divided. However, if you literally know the verse of the Qur'an, it says only guard your private parts. So there is no explicit verse in the Qur'an that says that masturbation is prohibited.

So what we understand from this is that a person is prohibited to have sex with anyone outside the marital bond. Allah, the Most Merciful and Wise, is talking only about adultery and nothing more.

Allah says in Surat Al-'Isrā' (The Night Journey), verse number 32, do not come close to adultery. It is an evil thing.

وَلَا تَقْرَبُوا۟ ٱلزِّنَىٰٓ إِنَّهُۥ كَانَ فَـٰحِشَةً وَسَآءَ سَبِيلًا ۝

And do not approach unlawful sexual intercourse. Indeed, it is ever an immorality and is evil as a way. (Qur'an 17:32)

Some scholars say that this verse specifically refers to sexual intercourse and nothing more. This means that sexual intercourse is only permitted with your spouse and with what your right hand possesses. It does not mean other things. Therefore if you agree with this, masturbation is not included in this verse as well.

This is the reason scholars differ and according to ibn Hasan (the great-grandson of the prophet), he said that our beloved prophet has permitted a person to touch his private parts. And in the hadith it says touch with your left hand no problem. It is your organ and you can touch it. He also said that it is your fluid and you can emit it if you want. So based on this, the prophet, peace and blessings be upon him, has permitted you to touch your private organ and that is what you do in masturbation, it is self-stimulation.

So surely it is permitted and masturbation is of two types, one it is only stimulation, and the other type of masturbation is with your spouse. And no scholar has ever said that your wife is not permitted to touch your private part. So based on this, your spouse is permitted to touch you. So if you enjoy this with your spouse, then why cannot you do it yourself. Some scholars say that this does not include masturbation at all. It is just talking about sexual intercourse. So sexual intercourse is only permitted with your wife. This is how the scholars differ.

Another argument given by some scholars who say that masturbation is prohibited, they mention the following hadith of the beloved Prophet, peace and blessings be upon him:

We were with the Prophet (peace and blessings be upon him) while we were young and had no wealth. So Allah's Messenger (peace and blessing be upon him) said, "O young people! Whoever among you can marry, should marry, because it helps him lower his gaze and guard his modesty (i.e. his private parts from committing illegal sexual intercourse etc.), and whoever is not able to marry, should fast, as fasting diminishes his sexual power." (al-Bukhari 5066, Book 67, Hadith 4)

So here the scholars say that the Prophet, peace and blessing be upon him, said if you cannot marry you should fast. However, the Prophet, peace and blessings be upon him, did not say masturbation. This is another reason that some scholars say that masturbation is haram.

However, since the Prophet, peace and blessings be upon him, said fast and did not say masturbate, this does not make masturbation haram. Yes what we have to understand from this hadith is that the young people should marry if they can. And if they cannot marry they should fast. This means fasting is mustahab (recommended), but no way does it mean that masturbation is haram.

Suppose I say that eating an apple is good for nourishment and for energy. So if the Prophet, peace and blessings be upon him, said to eat an apple, then this does not mean eating mangoes is haram. It only means that eating an apple is recommended. So fasting is more recommended than masturbation.

The other fruits become mubah so it is wrong to conclude from this hadith of Bukhari that masturbation is haram. It is wrong logic because for haram there should be strong evidence from the Qur'an or from say hadith.

So based on this, the second group of scholars who say it is not haram, they say there is no text at all anywhere in the Qur'an that say it is haram. And the only verse that the scholars quote from Surat Al-Mu'minun verse 5 to 7, they say it does not include masturbation. There is no clear-cut evidence it only speaks about sexual intercourse and there's no hadith prohibiting masturbation.

So we have come to the second group of scholars, and we will discuss what they say. They believe that masturbation is discouraged amongst them is Ibn Abbas. He was the companion of the prophet, peace and blessings be upon him. A person came to him and said, "I have been masturbating." Ibn Abbas said, "Masturbation is much better than fornication, but Marriage is always better." Then surely masturbation is permitted. However, if one is unable to fast or marry then they can masturbate because it will prevent them from fornication.

So based on this the second group of scholars who say masturbation is allowed, they say masturbation is still discouraged. That means it is discouraged but should not be avoided if it is done to prevent fornication. Jafar ibn Abi Talib said that there is no harm at all in doing it. There is no sin.

Imam Sha'rani also said masturbation is permitted. He was a distinguished writer. He produced works on a variety of subjects. He said that masturbation is optional if you want to do it, then do it. There is no sin at all. But he said that Masturbation is markuh but depending upon the situation.

So we have three groups of scholars. One group, (which is the majority) say it is haram based on the Qur'an and Surat Al-Mu'minun (23:5-7), whereas the second group of scholars say it is makruh. It is discouraged. But the third group said mubah. It is permissible and it all depends upon you.

According to me, being a medical doctor, in medical college, when I did my medicine, they used to say, when you ask a person if you masturbate 99% will say yes, and the remaining 1%, they are lying anyway. This is just a joke it is amongst the medical students, it is not a fact but according to research today, it entails, amongst the males 95% masturbate. Amongst the females, approximately 80% masturbate. I am not saying that it is normal to masturbate, but it is very common. There is a myth that, which is, if you go to some of the Islamic sites, those who believe in haram, masturbation causes blindness, and nervous problems. All these things are a myth, in no way does masturbation cause blindness or a nervous problem. If you do excessive masturbation then yes it can be problematic. Medical science tells us, if you do excessive sexual intercourse with your wife, (maybe 10 times a day) that will cause problems in the long run.

Anything extremely excessive can cause you problems. Normal masturbation medically does not cause any problems. If you masturbate according to medical science, it is normal. The majority of the people are involved in masturbation. I'm not saying it is the norm but I am saying that the majority of people do it.

So based on what the scholars say and what medical science is, I agree more with the second group of scholars and I would say masturbation is not a sin, but it is discouraged.

You are required to have strong evidence from the Quran or from hadith. There is no such evidence at all. So I do agree with the second group of scholars. It is not the act of nobility, but humans are still evolving. They are God's creatures and are not able to change the laws of nature.

Shaykh al-Islam Ibn Taymiyah was asked whether sin could be good for someone. Ibn Taymiyah said: *"Yes, with the condition that it is followed by being remorseful and repentant, by seeking forgiveness, and by being sincerely moved (to submission) on the inside."*

Allah (the Exalted) says: *And it may be that you dislike a thing that is good for you, and that you like a thing that is bad for you. Allah knows, but you do not know. And whosoever fears Allah and keeps his duty to Him, He will make his matter easy for him. (Qur'an 2:216, 65:4)*

In an authentic hadith, the Prophet (peace and blessings be upon him) relates this saying from Allah (the Exalted): *"I am with the thoughts of My slave towards Me, so let him think of Me as he pleases."*

فَقُلْتُ ٱسْتَغْفِرُوا رَبَّكُمْ إِنَّهُۥ كَانَ غَفَّارًۭا ۝

يُرْسِلِ ٱلسَّمَآءَ عَلَيْكُم مِّدْرَارًۭا ۝

وَيُمْدِدْكُم بِأَمْوَٰلٍۢ وَبَنِينَ وَيَجْعَل لَّكُمْ جَنَّٰتٍۢ وَيَجْعَل لَّكُمْ أَنْهَٰرًۭا ۝

Ask forgiveness from your Lord; verily, He is Oft-Forgiving. He will send rain to you in abundance; and give you increase in wealth and children; and bestow on you gardens; and bestow on you rivers. (Qur'an 71:10-12)

So seek forgiveness from Allah more often, and you will reap the benefits of doing so: peace of mind, lawful provisions, righteous offspring, and plentiful rain.

$$\text{وَأَنِ اسْتَغْفِرُوا رَبَّكُمْ ثُمَّ تُوبُوا إِلَيْهِ يُمَتِّعْكُم مَّتَاعًا حَسَنًا إِلَىٰ أَجَلٍ مُّسَمًّى وَيُؤْتِ كُلَّ ذِي فَضْلٍ فَضْلَهُ ۖ وَإِن تَوَلَّوْا فَإِنِّي أَخَافُ عَلَيْكُمْ عَذَابَ يَوْمٍ كَبِيرٍ ۝٣}$$

Seek the forgiveness of your Lord, and turn to Him in repentance, that He may grant you good enjoyment, for a term appointed. And that He may bestow His abounding grace to every owner of grace [that is, the one who helps and serves the needy and deserving, physically and with his wealth, and even with good words]. (Quran 11:3)

The Prophet (peace and blessings be upon him) said:

"Whosoever seeks forgiveness (from Allah) often, then Allah makes for him a good ending for every matter of concern and provides for him a way out of every tight situation."

Related in Bukhari is a hadith that is known as the chief of al-istighfâr [the supplications with which one asks Allah (the Exalted) for forgiveness]:

"O Allah, You are my Lord, and none has the right to be worshipped except You. You have created me and I am your slave; I am upon your covenant and promise as much as I am able to be. I seek refuge in You from the evil that I have perpetrated. I confess to You Your favor upon me, and I confess to You my sin, so forgive me; for verily, none forgives sins except You."

In Conclusion

Finally, Allah is the Most Merciful, and He always answers those who call on Him. So, by Allah's will, praying for forgiveness and assistance will be accepted.

Insha'Allah, this information will prove to be of some use to all Muslims. If there is any mistakes in what I have reported, may Allah forgive us; and whoever knows of the error, please inform us of it. With Allah is the guidance – May Allah guide us all.

Good Reads

Quran in Color	ISBN 9781643543987
Quran in Color	ISBN 9781643543994
Stories of the Prophets	ISBN 9781643544977
Stories of the Prophets	ISBN 9781643543703
Quran in English	ISBN 9781643543543
Quran Tafsir	ISBN 9781643544625
Sayings of the Prophet	ISBN 9781643544694
Ibn Al-Qayyim	ISBN 9781643543796
Don't Be Sad! Be Happy	ISBN 9781643544878
Noah's Stories of the Prophets - Bible and Torah	ISBN 9781643544847
Hadiths on Good Moral Values	ISBN 9781643544823
Matters of the Heart & Soul	ISBN 9781643544731

Battles of Prophet Muhammad ISBN 9781643544724

Stories of the Qur'an   ISBN 9781643544700

The Lofty Virtues of Shaykh al-Islam Ibn Taymiyyah

ISBN 9781643544601

Inner Dimensions of the Salah: Asrar Al-Salah (Prayer)

ISBN 9781643544571

The Journey of the Spirit after Death

ISBN 9781643544496

Timeless Seeds of Advice for the Muslima

ISBN 9781643544472

The Ídeal Muslímah   ISBN 9781643544458

Hadith of the Prophet   ISBN 9781643544366

Timeless Seeds of Advice to a Friend

ISBN 9781643544359

Muhammad: The Best Human Being of all Time

ISBN 9781643544342

Al-Husain Ibn Ali   ISBN 9781643544328

The Friends of Allah   ISBN 9781643544236

Gardens of Purification   ISBN 9781643544229

The Spiritual Cure   ISBN 9781643544212

Fleeing From the Fire   ISBN 9781643544205

My Africa   ISBN 9781643545004

www.ingramcontent.com/pod-product-compliance
Lightning Source LLC
Chambersburg PA
CBHW072212070526
44585CB00015B/1309